Think The Beautiful Thoughts

Thoughts

A Play for Women

Rae Shirley

A SAMUEL FRENCH ACTING EDITION

SAMUEL FRENCH

FOUNDED 1830

SAMUELFRENCH-LONDON.CO.UK
SAMUELFRENCH.COM

CAST in order of appearance:

MRS MORGAN	Aged about 70, deaf as a post but couldn't care less, she always seems to hear what she wants to hear and is invariably triumphant with the last word.
BESSIE	Her middle-aged married daughter. She likes having the last word as well - what woman doesn't - but, being no match for her mother, fights an eternally losing battle.
RACHEL MORRIS	A light-hearted widow with one ambition - not to remain a widow long!
CASSIE LEWIS	The traditional spinster of a certain age that is sometimes optimistically described as uncertain.
MADAME MARIE MORUZZIO	Fortune-teller par excellence; 'Visited by Royalty, Consulted by Princes.'

<u>Character and costume notes</u>

All the characters save MADAME MARIE have pronounced Welsh accents, and should be played with sincerity as they actually believe in the fortune-telling powers displayed. MADAME MARIE should have a not too obviously false foreign accent, French, Italian or Spanish for preference.

BESSIE and RACHEL dress to kill and, although CASSIE does her best, she still contrives to look old-fashioned and rather prim. She wears unbecoming spectacles and something resembling a school uniform (see play text).

MADAME MARIE although liberally bedecked with veils and shawls is an elderly lady. She fairly tinkles with beads and jewellery etc. and is most definitely 'an eccentric'. If the producer can suggest a veiled, mysterious 'presence' so much the better.

THINK THE BEAUTIFUL THOUGHTS *

Set: a comfortable living-room in BESSIE's house, furnished with a
few soft armchairs, four straight-backed dining chairs, a small
round table, the usual collection of small ornaments, photos etc.
Front door to street USR, door to kitchen SL. MRS MORGAN is seated in an armchair laboriously knitting what appears to be an inter-
minable scarf. She puts it down and looks around inquiringly:

MRS MORGAN   Very quiet it is for a Saturday afternoon. Yes ....
                very quiet. Nothing on television except old sport.
                Sport, sport, sport ..... that's all we get. Don't
                like it quiet like this, I don't. I know Emlyn's gore
                to the Rugby - Rugby mad he is - but where's that
                Bessie got to? (rising stiffly she goes to kitchen
                door SL and calls) Bessie! (louder) Bess - ie!
                ..... Never know where that girl gets to. Off, off,
                off, all the time she is - just like her father used to
                be. (sitting) Oh, well, better get on with this pull-
                over or it'll never be ready for Christmas......

                (BESSIE enters USR from street obviously dressed
                to kill and carrying a large bunch of flowers.)

                .... There you are at last, Bessie. Searched high
                and low for you, I have.

BESSIE   Mam! I haven't been gone five minutes.

MRS MORGAN   Five minutes! More like five hours.

BESSIE   I haven't got time to argue with you. You ready?

MRS MORGAN   Ready? What have I got to be ready for now, then?

BESSIE   Oh, Mam! If I've told you once I've told you a
                dozen times. You're having tea with old Mrs Watkins.

MRS MORGAN   Old Mrs 'oo?

---

*N.B. Paragraph 3 on page ii of this Acting Edition regarding
photocopying and video-recording should be carefully read.

BESSIE   Watkins, Mam, Watkins!

MRS MORGAN   (unimpressed) Oh - her! Talks too much she does.
                Can't get a word in edgeways.

BESSIE   (sotto voce) Makes a nice change for you, anyway.

MRS MORGAN   (sharply) What's that you said, Bessie?

BESSIE   (raising voice) I said it would be a nice change for
                you to go and have tea with her - that's what I said.

MRS MORGAN   You go. I'll stay here and wait for Emlyn.

BESSIE   Don't talk so daft, Mam. Emlyn won't be home for
                hours.

MRS MORGAN   What are you all dressed up for? Duw, she's off
                again.....

                (BESSIE is making SL for kitchen.)

                (loudly) Bessie! I'm speaking to you. Where're
                you off to now?

                (Exit BESSIE SL.)

                Bess - ie!

BESSIE   (entering SL carrying vase for flowers) For good-
                ness sake, Mam, can't I go and get a drop of water
                for the flowers without you blowing your top like a
                fire alarm!

MRS MORGAN   (worried) Fire alarm? What fire?

BESSIE   Mam! Where's your deaf-aid?

MRS MORGAN   In the fridge, of course!

BESSIE   (arranging flowers in vase, shrugging) I give up!

MRS MORGAN   (explaining) Always goes better after a spell in the

fridge. Very posh with those flowers, aren't we?
Expecting the minister to tea tomorrow?

BESSIE

No, I am not expecting the minister to tea tomorrow
but Mrs Watkins is expecting you to tea - today.
Come on, Mam. Let's get your hat and coat on.

MRS MORGAN

(not moving) There's something up. I can feel it
in my bones.

BESSIE

Feel it in your bones because you're going to have
tea with old Mrs Watkins?

MRS MORGAN

Because you're in such a stampede hurry to get me
out of here - that's why.

BESSIE

(innocently) I don't know what you're talking
about, Mam.

MRS MORGAN

To tell you the truth, neither do I.

BESSIE

Oh, Mam!

MRS MORGAN

(strongly) But I know there's something up. You
all dressed up like a dog's Christmas dinner and
fussing about with them flowers. How much did
they cost you?

BESSIE

It didn't come out of your pension so what are you
worrying about? Now, where's your hat and coat?
(exit quickly to kitchen SL)

MRS MORGAN

Just as well, my girl, or it's the last time you'll
be going to the post office for me. (realises that
she is talking to herself) Duw, she's gone again!
Can't pin her down for two minutes. Bess - ie!

(BESSIE enters SL with her mother's hat and coat.)

BESSIE

Here we are, Mam. Get moving.

MRS MORGAN

(not moving)   Don't you talk to me like that!

BESSIE

I said get moving, Mam. On your feet!

MRS MORGAN   (still seated) Cheek! That's all I get from her - sheer, unerduplicated cheek!

BESSIE   (plonking the hat on her mother's head at a rakish angle) Stand up and let's get your coat on.

MRS MORGAN   (rigid) Who's coming here this afternoon?

BESSIE   The Duke of Edinburgh! Come on, Mam, or I'm going to lose my temper.

MRS MORGAN   Lose your what?

BESSIE   (impatiently) Temper, Mam, temper!

MRS MORGAN   Temper? Temper is right! Like a bottle of pop she is.

BESSIE   Mam!

MRS MORGAN   Getting more like your father every day, you are. Like a flaming tiger he was when he got started. Ingrid, he'd yell at me - Ingrid -

BESSIE   (interrupting) - Yell at you? Mild as mother's milk our Dad was. It's you was the flaming tiger! (hauling her mother up) On with this coat - stick your arm in, will you? (after a struggle) Mam, you're not trying, are you?

MRS MORGAN   Not trying! You're breaking my arm - you know that, don't you? Not that you care! I'm only your poor old mother!

BESSIE   There .... that's got it! Now, come on, there's a good girl, and I'll walk you down to Mrs Watkins.

MRS MORGAN   Is my hat on straight?

BESSIE   (looking at the still rakishly angled hat) Straight enough for Mrs Watkins. Come on, Mam.

MRS MORGAN   (as they leave through front door USR) Come on, Mam, come on! That's all I get. Come on, Mam, come on. These youngsters! Come on, Mam, come on!

(The stage is deserted for a few moments then there
is a perfunctory knock on the front door followed
swiftly by the entrance of RACHEL and CASSIE, the
lively widow and her dim echo.)

RACHEL (breezily) No need to knock, Cassie. We saw
Bessie marching her mother down the street and
she gave us the nod to go in.

CASSIE (hanging back nervously) Well, we -er- sort of had
to observe the -er- what-d'you-call-it, didn't we?

RACHEL I wouldn't know what the what-d'you-call-it is, love.
Come on in. Make yourself at home. We have been
invited. you know. We're not housebreakers.

CASSIE Oh, I know that, Rachel. (wistfully) Smart costume
that is. New, isn't it?

RACHEL I'll say! Like it?

CASSIE Like it! I reckon you've got lovely taste, Rachel. I
never seen you yet in a costume I didn't like.

RACHEL Suit, Cassie, not costume. Costume's old fashioned.
(looking round room) Smashing flowers.

CASSIE Beautiful.

RACHEL Bessie must be expecting somebody important, I
reckon.

CASSIE I wonder what she wants us for. Do you know, Rachel?

RACHEL Haven't a clue. All she told me was to put my best bib
and tucker on and come round with 50p in my pocket.

CASSIE That's what she told me, too. I wonder what the 50p
is for?

RACHEL (in a serious tone) She likes cats. Maybe it's for a
cats' home.

CASSIE (astonished) Never! (anxiously) D'you reckon?

RACHEL   Don't be daft, Cassie. Don't you know when your leg's being pulled!

CASSIE   (sadly) That's my trouble. No sense of humour, Mam says. I reckon I'd have been married by now if only I'd had a sense of humour.

RACHEL   (taking out powder compact and studying her face in its mirror) And that's when you need it, love - when you're married.

CASSIE   I wouldn't know. You've been married twice, Rachel. Duw, that's what I call luck! How do you do it?

RACHEL   (busy applying make-up) All done with mirrors, Cassie.

CASSIE   I'm serious, Rachel.

RACHEL   So am I, love, so am I. (brandishing compact) Mirrors! Plus Woolworth's best. Making the most of this. (tapping face) It's hard work, damn hard work, if you'll pardon the expression - and you need to be careful.

CASSIE   Careful?

RACHEL   (searching in handbag) That's right. Never let them catch you off your guard. This bag! Where's my lipstick?

CASSIE   Off guard? What d'you mean?

RACHEL   Well ..... like bending over a hot stove in an old dress best cut up for dusters. Or caught answering the door with rollers sprouting from your head and your nose shining like red traffic lights. It's hard work, all right. Still, they're worth it, bless their drip-dry shirts. Life would be very dull without them.

CASSIE   (sighing) Life's dull for me, all right.

RACHEL   I hate to say this, Cassie, but it's not a bit of wonder, is it?

CASSIE (affronted) What's that supposed to mean?

RACHEL Nothing, love, nothing. You'll only get on that old
high horse of yours. (finds lipstick and applies it)

CASSIE No, I won't - honest. Tell me, Rachel.

RACHEL (dropping lipstick back into bag) Okay! (resignedly)
I'm probably putting paid to a beautiful friendship
so don't say you haven't been warned.

CASSIE Rachel!

RACHEL All right. Just take a look at yourself in cold blood.
Go on! Pretend you're somebody else looking at a
stranger. That blouse and thing like an old school
tie. You left school - how many years ago is it?
(as CASSIE attempts to answer) Never mind! I left
the same time, so I don't want to know...... but
the way you dress, you could still be in your old
gym-slip with those terrible navy-blue knickers.
By the way, do you still wear them?

CASSIE (shocked) Rachel!

RACHEL Well, that's something, anyway. I never even wore
the things in school........ Then there's those
glasses. Have you got to wear the things?

CASSIE I'm as blind as a bat without them.

RACHEL I'm blind as two bats - so what! Being short-sighted
gives you that helpless, innocent look. (snatches
glasses off CASSIE) That's better. Makes the men
feel strong and protective. Builds up their ego.

CASSIE I never thought of that.

RACHEL I have! You can see within three feet of you, can't
you?

CASSIE (doubtfully) Just about.

RACHEL   Well then, that's close enough to make your mind up about a man, isn't it?

CASSIE   (sadly) I wouldn't know. I've never been that close to any man.

RACHEL   Oh, I don't know - and they call this the permissive society! Here, let's have a go at you.

        (RACHEL removes CASSIE's tie, unbuttons her shirt into an enticing V neck and does her hair.)

CASSIE   (half protesting but not overdoing it) Rachel ...... what're you trying to do?

RACHEL   As if you didn't know! Giving you an instant do-it-yourself beauty treatment, that's what!

CASSIE   Oh dear! I feel sort-of bare.

RACHEL   (torn between exasperation and laughter) Bare - with two inches of skin showing! Now, let's have another look at you. Mmmm..... your eyes .... I know! A spot of eye-shadow. Makes all the difference.

CASSIE   Eye-shadow! Oh, no!

RACHEL   (delving into her bag) Oh, yes. Tch! The stuff I carry about with me ...... here we are......... (expertly putting the eye-shadow on her victim) Stop blinking, will you and keep still..... Still, I said...... There, that's more like it. (admiring her handiwork) Hmmm.... not bad. Not bad at all.

CASSIE   Let's have a look in your compact!....... O-ooh, Rachel! That's never me!

RACHEL   All done with mirrors, like I said. Treat yourself to a couple of see-through blouses and have a bit of pink ribbon showing through. That always gets them, a bit of pink ribbon. Fires their senses.

CASSIE   Fires their senses! Mam'll have a fit!

RACHEL Let her. It's you who wants to catch your man, not her. She's been married, hasn't she?

CASSIE Goodness, I hope so!

RACHEL That's right, then..... You got anyone special in mind?

CASSIE (coyly) We-e-eeell ......

RACHEL Don't come the shrinking violet with me, Cassie. 'smatter of fact, I've got a good idea who it is.

CASSIE You never! Who is it, then?

RACHEL Well, he's not six feet tall and he'll never see forty again!

CASSIE You're making fun of me.

RACHEL Of course I'm not. Nice little grocery business he's got, clean as a pin, and him always in a spot-less white apron.

CASSIE That's him - that's Willie Williams. You know?

RACHEL I know all right. I was watching him in chapel last Sunday night.

CASSIE (jealously) What were you watching him for?

RACHEL I was watching him watching you. I tell you now, Cassie, if you play your cards right, He's yours for the asking.

CASSIE D'you think so - honest? Oh, I hope you're right. I was afraid for a minute you had your eye on him.

RACHEL Not me, love..... I'm busy elsewhere.

CASSIE What - again? Who is it this time, Rachel?

RACHEL (confidentially) Promise me you'll keep it under your hat.

CASSIE   I won't breathe a word - not even to Mam.

RACHEL   Well, he's a retired police sergeant from Cardiff.
              A widower, no children, so the coast's clear.....
              Only one drawback ....

CASSIE   What's that?

RACHEL   (dead serious) He's English.

CASSIE   (equally serious) Oh? Never mind, girl. Some of
              them make good husbands, even if they are English.
              Has he said anything definite yet?

RACHEL   Not yet, but he's coming round to it. I know the
              symptoms. I've just bought myself this new rig-out
              and if this doesn't bring him to the boil, nothing
              will. Got a date with him tonight as a matter of fact.

CASSIE   Good luck, Rachel.

RACHEL   Ta, love..... and the same to you. Now don't go
              forgetting that pink ribbon - <u>under</u> the blouse.
              Guaranteed to set a man on fire.

CASSIE   (wistfully) I'd love to set Willie on fire.

RACHEL   You take my advice and it'll be a regular confla-
              gration!

              (BESSIE enters USR in a whirl.)

BESSIE   (breathlessly) Here I am at last! I thought I'd
              never get away from Mam. Talk the hind legs off
              a clockwork cow, she would. All I hope now is that
              she'll stay put with old Mrs Watkins and let us get
              on with it.

RACHEL   Get on with what, Bessie? What's all the mystery?

BESSIE   Let me get my breath back, will you? (looking at
              CASSIE) You look different, Cassie. What have
              you been doing to yourself? Look ten years younger,
              you do.

CASSIE   (overwhelmed) Oh, Bessie! Do you think so?

RACHEL   (impatiently) Don't change the subject, Bessie.
              Why did you ask us to come here?

BESSIE   You've got your 50 p's?

CASSIE
RACHEL   (together) Yes!

BESSIE   Hang on a minute,then,while I put the kettle on. My
              tongue's dropping out for a cuppa.

              (Exit BESSIE to kitchen SL.)

RACHEL   Talk about building up to a climax!

CASSIE   She's got a what-d'you-call-it? A sense of drama.

RACHEL   She's got something!

BESSIE   (entering) Only had to turn the gas on..... Now I
              can tell you everything.

RACHEL   And about time, too.

BESSIE   (ignoring her) Now, then, you two must have heard
              of the famous Madame Marie Moruzzio?

CASSIE
RACHEL   (together - emphatically) Never!

BESSIE   Don't you read the papers? Very famous she is.
              Visited by royalty! Consulted by princes!

RACHEL   (sceptically) Who says?

BESSIE   She says.

RACHEL   (sarcastically) Good for her!

BESSIE   (on the defensive) Everybody says!

CASSIE   What do they consult her about?

BESSIE   Everything.

RACHEL   (more sceptical than ever) <u>Every</u>thing?

BESSIE   You're a real pair of Doubting Thomases, aren't you? She tells fortunes, girl, fortunes! 50p a time.

RACHEL   Fifty pence! Is that what royalty pay her?

BESSIE   She's got a sliding scale .....

RACHEL   Some slide!

BESSIE   (delving into her bag) She's come on a flying visit to Wales.

RACHEL   On her broomstick?

BESSIE   (getting annoyed) Will you shut up, Rachel? (brings a visiting card out of bag) It says here she gives 'Private Sessions to Privileged People'.

RACHEL   And at 50p a time we're the 'Privileged People'?

BESSIE   Look, sarky, you enjoyed the fortune teller the last time we went to Blackpool, didn't you - the pair of you?

CASSIE   We did, you know, Rachel..... Do you reckon she'll see a husband for me, Bessie?

BESSIE   Stranger things have happened.

RACHEL   Now who's being sarky?

BESSIE   Kettle's boiling by now. I'm going to make that cuppa. (exit SL)

CASSIE   What do you think of it?

RACHEL   (still sceptical) I'll tell you afterwards.

(There is a knock on the front door and it is pushed
open almost immediately. MADAME MARIE enters,
she looks the eccentric which she undoubtedly is and
fairly tinkles with beads and jewelry of all descrip-
tions. Swathed in floating scarves etc.,she bows
ceremoniously to RACHEL and CASSIE. CASSIE
scrambles to her feet - followed less hastily by
RACHEL - and they bow awkwardly in return.)

MADAME M   (in a deep, sonorous voice) Grrr-eeee-tings!

CASSIE   (nervously) Er .... and the same to you.

RACHEL   Three bags full!

MADAME M   (advancing like a ship in full sail) Thrrr-eeeee
                bags full? You have the bags?

RACHEL   Every morning - under the eyes!

MADAME M   The English language - verrrr-ry, verry difficult.
                This is the abode of Madame Jon-ez?

CASSIE   (bewildered) Madame Jon-ez?

RACHEL   She means Jones, stupid. Yes, this is her abode.

MADAME M   Bon! All the little houses have the same door front.
                This is the third door front I have ker-nocked at.

CASSIE   She ker-nocked at three doors before coming here!

MADAME M   But yes .... and they were all calling themselves
                the family of Jon-ez.

                (BESSIE enters SL with the tea-tray. She stops dead
                when she sees the Apparition, who bows. BESSIE's
                attempts to follow suit are somewhat handicapped by
                the tray.)

                Grrrr-eeeee-tings!

BESSIE   Oh, yes, of course! Greetings!

RACHEL   (coming to the rescue) Can I give you a hand with
                the tea, Bessie?

BESSIE   Oh, yes, please.

MADAME M   The Brrrritttt-ish with their tea. Always their tea!

RACHEL   It's saved my life more than once!

BESSIE   Everybody take milk?

MADAME M   You have, please, the milk of the goat?

BESSIE   (flabbergasted) Milk of the goat? No, no milk of
                the goat. Milk of the cow, we got.

MADAME M   (firmly) The cow - she is not so clean as the goat.

RACHEL   (aside to CASSIE) She's got to be joking! Every
                goat I've met ponged to high heaven.

MADAME M   The sugar I take - but not the milk of the cow.

BESSIE   Here we are, then. One cup of tea, minus goat's
                milk - and cow's!

MADAME M   Merci. (sips tea) A-aah! The beautiful tea. It
                'elps the spirits and then the spirits, they 'elp me.

CASSIE   (nervously) Spirits? Does she mean g-g-ghosts?

RACHEL   Better ask her. Do you mean ghosts?

MADAME M   (sonorously) Ghooo-oosts? Ghoo-oosts? I do not
                know the ghooo-oosts. My spirit is Little Eskimo
                Guide.

BESSIE   Oh, my gawd!

MADAME M   He is charrrr-ming, so charrrr-ming! Sometimes
                a leeetle - dif-ferent. You know what Eskimos are.

RACHEL   (sotto voce) We've got a right one here!

MADAME M   His name – you will not be able to say it in the
             oreeeginal language – means Laughing Water. Such
             a charrrrming name. He pretends he is – how you
             say? – a fall of water .... waterfall.

CASSIE   Goodness!

MADAME M   So innocent.......

RACHEL   He'd better be! Laughing Water! Sounds like a
             Red Indian – you sure she knows what she's doing?

             (BESSIE looks daggers at RACHEL.)

MADAME M   ..... and before I look in the crystal ball, I have
             to first consult him.

BESSIE   You mean – you consult this Eskimo What's-'is-
             name before – ?

MADAME M   Every time.

CASSIE   (impressed) Goodness!

RACHEL   Ahem! Shall battle commence?

MADAME M   Before the commencing – first the business before
             the pleasure.

CASSIE   What's she on about now?

RACHEL   C.O.D. Cough up and deliver!

BESSIE   Oh, yes, of course. Fifty pence. Where's my bag?
             I'm forever losing the blessed thing – (finds it) oh,
             here we are.

MADAME M   (seer-like) Inflation is come.

RACHEL,CASSIE
& BESSIE   (together) Inflation?

MADAME M   Not fifty pence no more. Now it is seventy-five.

RACHEL   We should have known! Trust the Common Market!

                (They hand over the money. MADAME MARIE counts
                it carefully. BESSIE collects the tea cups.)

MADAME M   (counting) Ten... twenty...thirty... (mumbles to
                herself) Yes, we have the seventy-five pences. (to
                BESSIE) Now, a table before me, if you please.

                (BESSIE moves the small table to SC in front of
                MADAME MARIE. CASSIE and RACHEL move the
                four straight-backed dining chairs to positions in a
                half-circle around the table. MADAME MARIE sits in
                chair URC, indicating to BESSIE to sit SR of her.)

                Thank you.

                (BESSIE sits in chair with her back to the front door.
                CASSIE and RACHEL sit SL in front of kitchen door.)

                And now I am looking for my crystal ball.

                (MADAME MARIE delves into her old fashioned bag
                and searches fruitlessly. She turns out her pockets
                and returns to the bag. Turning this out reveals
                such diverse items as a pack of Tarot cards, dice,
                huckle-bones, an astroscope, bell, book and candle,
                pocket guides to Astrology, Astronomy, Necromancy,
                Astragalomancy and 'Table-turning for Beginners'.
                Also hidden in a corner of the voluminous bag is the
                crystal ball wrapped in black velvet. Throughout
                this performance BESSIE, RACHEL and CASSIE have
                been gazing at her in wide-eyed astonishment.)

                (pouncing on crystal ball triumphantly) Aaaah!
                'iding 'imself! (polishes ball vigorously then sets
                it in middle of table) Always he is 'iding 'imself.
                Now .... I am popping into the trance.

CASSIE   Popping into the trance?

RACHEL   Let her get on with it, for gawd's sake, or we'll be
                here all night.

MADAME M   (producing a veil from pocket) Now I am placing
                the ectoplasmic veil over the face - so! (drapes
                veil over her head)

RACHEL   (in sheer disbelief) Ectoplasmic my -

MADAME M   (lifting veil and peering out) And now I am going
                to pop!

                (MADAME MARIE replaces veil, leans back in her
                chair and relaxes with a sigh. She is soon breathing
                heavily, the veil lifting slightly at first then, as her
                breathing intensifies, it starts billowing upwards.
                CASSIE, RACHEL and BESSIE all watch fascinated.)

RACHEL   (to BESSIE) You seen her in action before?

BESSIE   (curtly) No.

CASSIE   She's a bit - er - what-d'you-call-it? You know
                what I mean ..... isn't she?

BESSIE   (coldly) I don't know what you mean, a bit what?

CASSIE   Well ... you know .... funny.

RACHEL   Funny? She's a flaming riot!

CASSIE   (bending anxiously towards MADAME MARIE) She's
                snoring.

RACHEL   I've got ears!

BESSIE   If she doesn't get a move on, we'll have Mam
                barging in and spoiling everything.

RACHEL   (looking at watch) I've got a date in Cardiff tonight.
                (leaping up with a sudden wild scream) Ooooooooch!
                Oooooooh!

BESSIE   What the - has she gone bonkers?

RACHEL   Somebody's pinching my - ooooooooh - ooooooooh!

CASSIE   Don't talk so daft, girl.There's nobody here to –
              (also leaping up) Ooooooh! Oooooooooooh!

              (RACHEL and CASSIE are clinging together for
              support.)

BESSIE   (also rising and shaking MADAME MARIE) Oh, my
              gawd! I'd better wake her before – Madame Mor-
              uzzio, Madame Moruzzio! Wake up, wake up!

MADAME M   (awakening and removing the veil from her face)
              Aaaah! Now I am ready for the – Ladies! For why
              are you making the embrace?

RACHEL   (letting go of CASSIE and resuming seat) We were
              not making the embrace. I reckon your Little
              Laughing Water was trying to be funny.

MADAME M   (fondly) Aaah, that naughty little one! Always he
              is playing the little trickses. Ahem! Now, to work.
              Who is liking to be first with their fortune? Ladies?
              First to go, please.

RACHEL   (as neither of the others seems anxious) I'm game!

MADAME M   Bon! Now, you will please to hold the crystal ball
              in the 'and – so – and think the beautiful thoughts.

              (Tentatively RACHEL takes the ball and rolls it
              around in her hands.)

              Now we must all think the beautiful thoughts.

              (They all assume beatific expressions, eyes
              heavenwards. There is a slight pause, then the
              atmosphere is broken by CASSIE hiccoughing.)

CASSIE   Hic! Pardon me!

BESSIE   (having almost lost the spirit of the thing) All I hope
              is that Mam don't march in or she'll give us
              beautiful thoughts!

MADAME M   (ignoring BESSIE and CASSIE) Now, we are ready.

(Taking crystal ball from RACHEL, MADAME MARIE
passes her hands over it in a mysterious abraca-
dabra fashion.)

Ah! (gazing passionately into its depths) In-ter-
rrresting! Verr-y, verr-y in-ter-rrresting!

BESSIE   Sounds interesting!

MADAME M   I see .... I see ..... a man!

RACHEL   (hancing on every word) A man?

MADAME M   A man.

RACHEL   Only one?

MADAME M   Not to interrupt, please! Ahem .... I see a man..
                .... I see - two men! I see - can it be possible?
                Three men!

RACHEL   (archly) It's possible.

MADAME M   A-a-aaah, yes. Two ....yes, two of the gentlemen
                are in the Great Beyond - where there are no more
                insurance claims.

BESSIE   We've heard of it!

MADAME M   (still gazing raptly at the ball) You have been
                lov-<u>ed</u>.

RACHEL   (eagerly) Yes, yes!

MADAME M   And I think I see - without a doubt - you will be
                lov-<u>ed</u> again.

RACHEL   Yes, yes?

MADAME M   I see ..... a tall man. Strong, strong as a moun-
                tain lion in his prime!

CASSIE   (breathlessly) Ooooooh!

RACHEL   Be quiet, Cassie! This is my fortune, not yours.

MADAME M   I see something flashing - flashing and bright. Can
                it be - is it possible? Diamonds?

RACHEL   (thrilled) Diamonds?

MADAME M   I look again. Aaaah! It is not diamonds, it is the
                brass buttons.

RACHEL   (deflated) Oh! Them!

MADAME M   Now the buttons fade away........

CASSIE   (in an audible whisper) Your retired police ser-
                geant.

RACHEL   Shut up!

MADAME M   The crystal ball is fading ... but ... wait a minute!
                A ring! I see a ring!

RACHEL   (triumphantly) I knew it!

CASSIE   Some girls get all the luck!

MADAME M   You would like to ask one question, yes?

RACHEL   I'd like to ask a couple.

MADAME M   (firmly) One only. It is seventy-five pennies you
                are paying, not seventy-five pounds.

RACHEL   When do I get this ring?

MADAME M   (studying hard) The stars say - in a three......

RACHEL   Three days, three weeks, three months?

MADAME M   The picture is going ... going.....

RACHEL   (delving into purse) Wait a minute, wait a minute!
                Here's another seventy-five pence.

MADAME M	(taking the money) Already the picture returns. (peering into ball) Three months only. Before Christmas comes you will be walking up the aisle. I see ... I see one big stocking and one small stocking hanging on one big, beeeeg double-bed.
RACHEL	(sighing) It was worth a bit extra to hear that!
CASSIE	My turn now.
BESSIE	What about me? I'm the one who brought her here.
RACHEL	Come on, Bessie - give Cassie a break.
BESSIE	All right, then, but don't be too long or Mam'll be back and spoil everything.
MADAME M	Are we all 'appy?
RACHEL	(beaming) I am!
MADAME M	(handing CASSIE the ball) If you will please to take the instrument and pass on your aura.
CASSIE	Pass on my what?
MADAME M	Your aura.
CASSIE	I never knew I had one.
BESSIE	Me, neither. What is it?
MADAME M	It is your electrical repulsion.
CASSIE	Mẏ gawd!
MADAME M	Concentrate, please, and think the beautiful thoughts.
	(CASSIE closes her eyes, rolling the ball in her hands.)
	You are thinking the beautiful thoughts?
	(CASSIE nods her head with gusto.)

	Good, very good. (takes ball back and passes hands over it à la abracadabra) Aaah! (peers closer) Aaaaaah! Aaaaaaah! (rising crescendo) Aaaaaaah!
CASSIE	(nervously) Wha- what is it?
MADAME M	I see a large crowd..... many, many peoples.
RACHEL	Tesco's on a Friday!
CASSIE	(reproachfully) Rachel! I never made fun of you when you were having your fortune told.
RACHEL	Can't you take a joke?
CASSIE	Not in the middle of my fortune.
MADAME M	(sternly) When you make the funny joke, you spoil the beautiful thoughts, so do not make the funny joke, eh?
CASSIE	She won't do it again.
MADAME M	(returning to ball) Aaah - here is something... all white... whiter than the snow on the mountain-top.
BESSIE	Oh, Duw! A ghost!
MADAME M	I look again. (shakes her head) Too fat he is for a ghost. Too short and too fat. Aaah! He is speaking something. What is he speaking?
CASSIE	Tell me, tell me!
MADAME M	(intoning) Half a pound of butter and a quarter of tea. Will that be all, madam?
CASSIE	(tremulously) Willie Williams!
RACHEL	That's Willie Williams all right. Short and fat in his whiter than white apron.
CASSIE	Is that all he says? Half a pound of butter and a quarter of tea?

MADAME M   That is all what his lips say - but his 'eart go pit-a-pat, pit-a-pat!

CASSIE   O-ooooh!

MADAME M   I see an 'igh cliff......

CASSIE   (staggered) A high cliff?

MADAME M   A beeg jagged mountain. Ah, I 'ave seen it before. It is the famous Leap of the Lovers.

BESSIE   Lovers' Leap!

CASSIE   Oh, Duw, what am I doing up there? Can't stand heights, I can't.

MADAME M   Nothing. You are not there. Nobody is there. Only the sheep.

CASSIE   But - but what about Willie?

MADAME M   Weelie?

CASSIE   The gentleman in white. Is he going to ask me a question?

MADAME M   (peering again) I do not .... no, no. He will not ask you a question.

CASSIE   (shattered) Oh!

MADAME M   You - you are going to ask the question. (with emphasis) The question.

CASSIE   (overcome) Me - ask him? Oh, no, no! Not me! Never! I could never!

MADAME M   You could - and you will. That is the symbolical of the Leap of the Lovers. It is Leap Year - and you ask him.

RACHEL   You're a sly one, too, Cassie.

CASSIE   And - and what does Willie say?

MADAME M   (peering) He say - nothing.

CASSIE   (dismayed) Nothing?

MADAME M   He embraces you to his white apron.

CASSIE   (ecstatically) At last!

MADAME M   And wedding bells in a two.

CASSIE   In a two - what?

MADAME M   Time will show.

BESSIE   My turn now, Cassie.

CASSIE   I wouldn't mind paying a bit more for a bit extra.

BESSIE   There isn't time, I tell you. Mam will be back any
            minute and then I'll have had my chips.

MADAME M   Madame Bessie is ready?

BESSIE   Madame Bessie is ready.

MADAME M   Bon! Take please the instrument and everybody -
            (looking round at them) everybody think the beau-
            tiful thoughts.

            (BESSIE takes the crystal ball and all four assume
            rapt expressions gazing heavenwards, concentrating
            on the beautiful thoughts. The front door opens USR
            and MRS MORGAN enters unobserved. She takes in
            the scene with the knowing eye of experience and
            approaches BESSIE and gives her an almighty jab in
            the back. BESSIE drops the crystal ball on the floor
            and lets out a horrified yell.)

BESSIE   Ooooooh! (turning) Mam!

MADAME M   (horrified) The instrument, the instrument!

MRS MORGAN   Who the heck's she? Gypsy Rose Lee!

BESSIE   (on knees searching) Never you mind who she is.

MADAME M   (desperately) The instrument, the instrument!

MRS MORGAN   What's she on about? What instrument?

               (RACHEL and CASSIE are peering anxiously under
               the table. BESSIE, still on her knees, is frantically
               searching for the ball.)

BESSIE   Her crystal ball, Mam, her crystal ball!

MRS MORGAN   (astounded) Crystal ball? Did you say crystal ball?

BESSIE   (yelling) Yes! Crystal ball!

MRS MORGAN   The way that girl yells at me, you'd think I was deaf,
               indeed to God you would!

BESSIE   Here it is! (emerges from under table) Duw!

               (BESSIE places ball on table. MADAME MARIE goes
               to pick it up but she is beaten to it by MRS MORGAN.)

MADAME M   (excitedly) Give it to me! Give it to me!

MRS MORGAN   (tossing it to her) Here, have it you!

MADAME M   Mon dieu! She tosses it like a ball for the cricket.

MRS MORGAN   You've been having your fortune told again, Bessie?

BESSIE   (bitterly) I've been trying to!

MRS MORGAN   I knew there was something up, see? I felt it in my
               bones, I did. (looking at MADAME MARIE) She's a
               new one, isn't she? (sits in BESSIE's chair)

MADAME M   (regally) I am Madame Marie Moruzzio. Visited
               by royalty. Consulted by princes.

MRS MORGAN   And I'm Elizabeth Taylor and if Richard Burton was
                here, he'd laugh in your face!

BESSIE   (aghast) Mam!

MADAME M   What did the old one say?

MRS MORGAN   (belligerently) <u>What</u> did she call me?

RACHEL   (half getting-up) I think we'd better be going.

CASSIE   (nervously, following suit) Yes, I think we'd better.

MRS MORGAN   Don't be daft, girls. Sit down, sit down. You
                can't go without having a cup of tea. Bessie! You
                know where the kettle is. (leans towards MADAME
                MARIE and stares at her face) Your face ...... it
                reminds me of someone ..... on the tip of my –

MADAME M   (interrupting, trying to brave it out) Impossible,
                madame! I am on a flying visit to –

MRS MORGAN   (imperturbably carrying on) – Maggie Jenkins her
                name was. Nice girl. A bit younger than me, but
                not much. She used to play around with a bit of
                fortune-telling. Tea-leaves it was then, though, not
                crystal balls. Big pals we were, till she up and mar-
                ried a Frenchman .... wounded soldier he was.
                (leans forward confidentially to MADAME MARIE)
                You remember Ingrid Evans, don't you, girl?

MADAME M   (dropping foreign accent, delightedly) Ingrid! It's
                never **you**!

MRS MORGAN   Course it's me, girl. How's it going, Maggie?

RACHEL   Well, I'll be – We've been had!

MRS MORGAN   (sharply) You mind what you're saying, Rachel
                Edwards. Best fortune-teller in the valley, Maggie
                was. Said to the day when I was going to marry Ivor –
                and about me only going to have one child – her!

BESSIE   (interrupting) Mam, it's my turn next!

MRS MORGAN   (ignoring her) Tell me, Maggie, what about it, eh?
               Any surprises left for me?

MADAME M   (picking up crystal ball) We'll soon see, Ingrid -
               (hands her ball with usual business and reassumes
               accent) now, take the crystal ball and think the
               beautiful thoughts - everybody, think the beautiful
               thoughts!

               (They all follow MADAME MARIE's instructions,
               beautiful thoughts fairly oozing from them; all, that
               is apart from BESSIE who is doing her best to break
               the air of concentration.)

BESSIE   Ma-am! I told you once! It's my turn next, I tell
               you - it's my turn!

               (All ignore BESSIE's outburst as the curtain descends
               on the tableau of women; all, save BESSIE, assuming
               rapt expressions, eyes heavenwards. BESSIE throws
               them a bitter and expressive look.)

CURTAIN

MADE AND PRINTED IN GREAT BRITAIN BY
LATIMER TREND & COMPANY LTD, PLYMOUTH
MADE IN ENGLAND

www.ingramcontent.com/pod-product-compliance
Ingram Content Group UK Ltd.
Pitfield, Milton Keynes, MK11 3LW, UK
UKHW021820150726
7214IPUK00017B/238